Human Noise

Poetry of

───────

Lauren Waites

Mission Viejo, CA
OC Poetry Club Press
2016

Human Noise
Copyright © 2016 by Lauren Waites

All rights reserved. No part of this book may be reproduced or transmitted in any form or by any means without written permission from the author.

ISBN-13: 978-1537028422
ISBN-10: 1537028421

Printed in the USA by OC Poetry Club Press

Dedicated to every adult who forgets they were once children.
And to my parents, for never allowing their youth to escape them.

Table of Contents

As we are Now	9
Vincent Van Gogh Find Yourself	12
Open Letter	15
Porch Light	16
Predisposed Surrender	17
This Life	18
If I Ruled the World	20
Shutter	23
Secret War	24
Being as an Ocean	25
Just like Wind	29
Snapshot	30
Of Flaws we are Created	34
Ethel	37
What they Don't tell you	39
Coughing Up Blood	40
Human Noise	41

"I could hear my heart beating. I could hear everyone's heart. I could hear the human noise we sat there making, not one of us moving, not even when the room went dark."

-What We Talk About When we Talk About Love,
Raymond Carver

As We Are Now

A kid who sits two rows behind me in my remedial math class says
he wants to be a Cardiothoracic surgeon.
No one has the
heart to tell him.
It doesn't have to make sense,
it just has to be real.

If you give someone a TigerLilly, you're saying,
"I dare you to love me."
Don't mention the part about how deadly
This lily is to anything who might eat it.
If you give someone a Tigerlily, you're saying,
"I dare you to love me
Even though I am toxic
to your system."

It doesn't have to make sense,
it just has to be real.
I knew a girl in the eighth grade who said she was scared to death
that she would never
be afraid of death.

I noticed a few years back
that there are certain parts
of my backyard
That never feel the scorch
of the sun.
The only thing these square inches of concrete know
is that they have always
been a safe haven
for burning feet in the summertime.
The only thing I know
is that I will never
have friends like
the ones I had during
The summer of 2010.

It's strange to think of
your life as seasons.
To think of how happy
you were then
versus how happy
you aren't anymore.
It doesn't have to make sense,
it just has to be real.

We all like to wonder
how many people it takes
to change a lightbulb,
but no one's ever asked
how many lightbulbs
it takes to change people.
Because I see a lot
Of humans
But no humanity.
I see society
But no community.
I see a lot
Of lovers
But no love.
It doesn't have to make sense,
it just has to be real.

It doesn't have to be real.
It doesn't have to be real.
It doesn't have to be real.
It just
Has to mean something
To someone.

Vincent Van Gogh Find Yourself

But no matter how hard we tried,
We could never find anything
As beautiful as the sun.
And we never heard anything
Quite like the
Sound of the rain
Patting against the unpaved roads
Like it was speaking to us
In morass code.
Our legs that always seems to wander
Slightly off track
And our minds that wandered a little more than slightly.

We don't know who we are
Because everyone's always told us who
We should be.
They called us
The Lost Boys and Girls
But we knew
We were so much more than that.
We were soldiers.
Obstacles.
We were the
Out-of-nowhere thunderstorm,
The wet socks
On a sunny day.
We were oddities who
Didn't have a house
So we made the street corners and
Deserted sidewalks our homes.
Begging for money
Wherever we could
And searching for a savior.
We didn't believe in God or the devil,
We believed in the kindest
Of strangers.

We depended on the stars
To find our way back to each other
And we punched holes in walls
To rid ourselves
Or everything
That ever
Held us back.

We don't make a difference
In this world,
We fill in,
It's what we were born to do.
We learned the hard way
That life doesn't stop for anyone,
You'll find us
In the cracks in the road.
The bystanders to semi beautiful events,
The people you forgot you met,
What's your name again?
We don't need to be noticed
And we don't need to be remembered.
But if you're looking
You'll know where to find us.

We'll be on a world tour
Broadcasting that
We were here.
We rested
In abandoned apartment buildings
And went to funerals
For people we never knew.
The traveled this continent
By foot,
Knees,
And by thumb.
We are hypocrites in the
Teaching.
We live vicariously through

Stories that should not be funny
And we swore to
The younger versions of ourselves
That we would change something
Someday.

But we woke up late.
That Sunday was yesterday
The sun was
Our only alarm clock
And we followed the lead of our parents.
How many
Of our parents
Even make it
Anyway?
We gave up.
But that's no where we went wrong.
We went wrong believing
That we were supposed
To be the hero.
We never actually found the person we should've saved,
We didn't know we were
Expected to save ourselves.

This is why we laugh
At the people we see
Who've got sidewalks
More passionate than them.
They meander around
With their chests out
And perfectly
Performed strides.
They buy houses to make up for
The lack of a home
And walk right past
The family begging for
Money on the corner,
Begging for a home in the corner.

The truth is,
I think we're jealous
Of them.
You see, we are
The family begging for
Money on the corner
And all that money could've
Been used to fee half of our population.
We chase waves in our
Veins to remember
The way the ocean tastes.
Recite battered memories
From our old
Favorite movies
And the times when we
We're still young enough to
Remember to blink
Periodically.
This the science of our existence.

We're not crazy,
We've just
Forgotten who we are for
A little bit.
But don't worry
One day we'll be just
The way you want us to be.
Like you, and like he.
You see, it's all an art.
We just paint
A little slower
Than the rest.

Open Letter

Some time ago,
I wrote a letter to god.
And in this I asked her
Him,
Them,
The questions
I had always wanted to know.
But at the end of it all,
I erased everything from the page
And just wrote the word,
"Why"

Porch light

We leave the lights on
When we can't sleep at night,
In hopes that someone
Who has the same dilemma
Will walk past,
See the signal
That only the lonely understand,
Shout from the porch and say,
"Hey. Me too!"

And it is in this hope,
This irrational hope,
That we leave lights on,
And that we go to bookstores,
And coffee shops,
And the reason we travel,
Because we're searching for love.
And the lover we are supposed to have
Will have the same hiding spots
As us.

So we leave the light on.

Predisposed Surrender

All these kids with
pants too big and
old worn out hats.
Women who smell of burnt hair
and cheap perfume
roam the churches
looking for God knows what.
All of their knees are bruised
from the times they spent praying on things that never came,
things that never come.

This Life

It's the way it feels
To roll the windows down
As the sun is rising
Over the horizon on the
East side of the world.

It's the sound of coffee
Drip drip dripping
Into the pot
When your lover can't sleep at night.

It's the way it feels
To step out of a too-hot shower
Into the cold chill
Of morning.

It's in the faint flicker
Of a candle that you know
Is burning out.
It's the faint flicker
Of a love that you know
Is wearing down.

It's stepping out of a car
That's still moving slightly
And feeling a strange
Rush of excitement.

It's the way it feels to
Hold someone's hand
For the second time.
Unsure, timid, anxious.

It's wearing new shoes
And trying not to crease them.
It's wearing old shoes

And trying to remember
Every memory
Held within them.

It's the last kiss
Before you break up.
Not fully knowing
It's the last kiss
Before you break up.

It's the soft murmur of night
After finishing a book.

It's Crying and
Singing and
Dancing and
Laughing and
Loving and
Crying and
Loving and
Wishing and
Hoping and
Losing.

If I Ruled the World

If I ruled the world,
Mosquitos wouldn't exist.
I'd visit all the homeless men and women,
All the corner tenants
Battling between starvation and addiction,
I'd go back in time
To take the syringe out of their palms,
I'd travel back twenty years,
Back before they knew they were decaying.
I'd put grand thoughts
In their heads,
I'd put A's on all their report cards,
I'm un-breaking their hearts
And never allowing them to
Learn the word "loss".
I'd give them
Livable wages so that
They'll never have to know
What cold concrete feels like against their bare chest.

And if I ruled the world,
I'd make the bad times pass quickly
and the good ones slow down a little bit. Quite the opposite
of what we know to be reality,
isn't it?
If I ruled the world
id turn all the clocks sideways.
Let's rejoice at midnight
and lay to rest at sunrise.
Make us all into night owls
with whoo whoo who
what when where and why
will never be questions asked
but rather answered.

And if I ruled the world

I'd turn suicide notes into campfires,
throw them out windows
and yell "you ain't gotta go home!
But you gotta get the hell! Outta! Here!"
I'd take Benadryl and Xanax
and grind them into the concrete,
I'll never let you learn
the word escapism.
No more ADHD or PTSD.
Shoot your demons
in the dark and always
hit right on the mark.
This is no longer a nightmare honey,
we're turning fear into art.

And if I ruled the world,
We'd splatter it in pinks and purples and blues and oranges,
The sky will always look like
An LA sunset and it will never
Get less beautiful.
And if I ruled the world you would know
That you were beautiful.
You, girl, are beautiful.
You, grandma, are beautiful.
You…sir, are beautiful.

And if I ruled the world
We'd all learn to play the tambourine
Because it's the easiest
Instrument to play and,
We all deserve a little music from time to time.
If I ruled the world
Beyoncé would never die
And Donald trump would have
Never been born.

If i ruled the world,
Our veins would look like New York City.

Busy and bustling and always
Pulsing. Pulsing. Pulsing. With life.
And if I ruled the world
I'd throw my nikes in the ocean and say
I'm not running anymore!".
Give the fish some shoes
and maybe we would stop killing them.
If I ruled the world
we would stop killing them.
If I ruled the world
 we would stop killing each other.
If I ruled the world
we would stop killing ourselves.

Shutter

There's silence
when you're surrounded
by things of beauty.
Everyone's a little bit
afraid to move
and all of a sudden
you hear the shutter of a camera.
The silence is broken.
You can breathe now.

Secret War

We are slow,
And we are rigid,
And we are breaking.

We are
Breaking hearts,
And breaking backs,
And cracking knuckles,
And getting ready for the fight.

We are squaring up
And stepping down.

This is us
Convincing ourselves
That we will never amount to anything.
This is us
Digging our graves
Because we believe it to be true.

This is the apocalypse,
And we aren't opting to survive.

Being as an Ocean

Raise your shaky hand if
You are a girl and shout
"I am here! I am here!"
Because you know what it is
To have your voice get lost
In the thunder.
To have it drained
By the constant noise
Of the pull and the push
Of the ongoing waves.
In the ebb of the "sit downs",
In the flow of the
"Only speak when spoken to,"
"Only talk when talked at,"
In the utter fear of tsunami's
Overcoming your body
And you want to shout
"I am here!"
"I am here!"
But there is no use,
Because you know that
No matter how loud your voice gets,
You will never be more powerful than the ocean.

Girl,
You are more
Than what you are not.
And girl,
You are not afraid.
So girl,
You do not need to be
A poem to be beautiful,
And girl,
You do not need to be
An ocean to be noticed.
So make sure all the

Submarines you send to explore
Your uncharted waters
Are verified and able
To handle whatever hidden waves
They might find within you.
Make sure they know
That you have been gutted
Of your childhood by
"Hey pretty girl,
Why don't you smile?"
Tell whomever it is
That is brave enough to go on an adventure
That you've got some dark parts
In the pit of your being
That haven't seen the light
In a while.
Tell them,
When too many planes
Have come crashing from the sky,
A few
Hundred passenger cruise ships
Thought they were going on vacation
But found themselves lost in the middle
Of despair instead.

Make sure you tell the world
That you will never stop sending
Hurricanes of emotions,
Nor tsunami's of anger and rage.
Make sure the news forecasters know
That they've got a big storm coming,
Because you have been quiet
For too long and you are shouting,
"I am here!"
"I am here!"
Make sure they know
That you've got a lot of missing parts,
But that you

Are not an endangered species
And you
Are not a quiet one either.
Make sure they know
That they can not send out a rescue boat
To come and save you
Because you
Are not to be saved
By them.

And "Dear world,"
You will write,
"World,
Even though I am only making
Seventy-seven cents
To a man's one-hundred,
I will never be afraid
To give my all.
I will never be afraid
To get my one-hundred and ten.
So world,"
You will say,
"World,
Throw it all out there,
Lay it all on me,
I am girl
And I am here!
I am here!"

When I gave in,
I was a survivor,
And when I fought back,
I was a warrior.
And for every woman that did
None of the above,
And for every woman
That did both,
For every girl,

A silenced dream,
For every wave crashing with
Fire and anger and fight and flee,
You. Are. Enough.

So girls,
Raise your glasses,
Raise your tides,
And raise your voices.
Let's toast
To this lifelong storm.
And let's storm
Out of every room and conversation
Where someone tells us,
That we
Have too much vigor.
That we
Have too many unchartered waters
And not enough survivors.
Raise your hand
If you are a girl
And you refuse to apologize
For all of those
Who have been darkened by your light.
If you have been made
To feel bad
About the vastness of your soul,
Or the beasts
That live under your surface.
Because I know
That there is not a single person alive
Who is not at least
A little bit afraid
Of the ocean.

Just like the Wind

I held you
For no more than
A small wisp of time.
And yet,
That is still enough
To last me
An eternity.

Snapshot

I used to take pictures
of everything.
Sidewalk gum,
people smiling,
people crying,
people laughing,
old men in tank tops,
you know, just life things.

I would take pictures
of everything.
Every moment,
every muse.
Every good deed,
every gust of bad luck.
And really,
this is all we have
to hold on to.
These memories held in time
in still pixels
that reveal who we were
in that moment
that didn't know…blank.
For example,
who was I when I was six
that didn't know
that most of the stars in the sky
are already dead?
Who was I in the fourth grade
That didn't know
that math would one day
contain the alphabet?
Who was I then
that didn't know
that we would all eventually die?
You know, just life things.

Now that I know
that the night sky
illuminates old flames,
I work hard not to
illuminate old pains.
Now that I know
that math contains letters,
I write poetry
On the back of tests.
Now that I know
I'm going to die,
I live.
Because I heard
About the
Red string of fate,
And I want to test
Its durability.
Tie it around every relationship
Twice.
Weave it through laughter
And combust it with every firework.
Let it be known
That I've dragged it through hell and back.
Let it be known
That when I get to where I'm going
I'll have snapshots
Of my life lived,
Wrapped around my finger.

We all want to
Make it to the end
Knowing that we fought the whole way.
So we shock stories into our systems
with adrenaline
and sweaty palms,
we skydive and bungee jump,
and climb Mount Everest.

We take pictures
of people laughing until they cry
and of people crying until they dry sob.
We tickle
to the point of pain
and we dye our hair
and fall in love.
Because this is what it means
to be alive.
This is what it means
to be human on purpose.
This is learning
that pavement cracks
and this is realizing
that people do, too.
This is shattering on accident
and having the courage
to put yourself back together
On purpose.
This is me
dropping my camera
and seeing the world
through a bigger lens.

Every still frame
now has a glitch
straight down the middle,
every life
now split in two parts;
who you are
and who you long to be.
And if these glitches
mean anything to you,
If these pictures hold
Any stories within you,
let it be this;
who we were in those moments
that did not know

what it meant to be alive,
is not who we are now.
And that's the glitch in the matrix,
that's the difference
between living and surviving.
That's the difference
Between a clean thread
And one you're proud to say
Has been ripped and torn so many times
We almost doubted its ability
To withstand.

And that's the reason
we go on road trips
and sing at the top of our lungs
and take pictures of people
smiling and laughing
because if this red string
Is as durable as they say it is,
Then I'll get to where I'm going
Anyway.
So I'll take a snapshot,
I'll take a screenshot,
I'll take a gunshot wound to the heart.
I'll die with stories
Trickling out of my system
And that red string of fate
Trailing behind me.
And when I die,
Let it be known
That I lived.

Of Flaws we are Created

We forget what we are made
until we look up into the sky
and our soul
escapes us for a while
because it wants to go home.
We want to go home.

Our biggest human flaw
is making a home
in the eyes of strangers
and pretending we see
God in them too.
Our biggest human flaw
Is being held for so long
That we begin to forget
That we once stood
On our own.
It's seeking safety in numbers
And seeking safety in others
And standing alone
And being alone
And yet still saying,
"I refuse to move"
And yet still saying,
"I deserve more than this".

Because when someone
That you love
Begins to tear at your muscle,
Begins to rip away
The years and years of
Fight, of anger, of frustration,
When someone that you love
Begins to treat you
As if they don't,
Begins to pick-pocket you

Of your confidence,
And rob you of your voice,
It happens
When you begin to write
The antagonist of your story
As your lover,
When you forget to
Write yourself as the protagonist.
It happens
When this love tastes like
Iron and whiskey,
Cuts like copper ,
And diminishes like your spirit.
You forget to wear the cape,
You forget to be your hero.

This compost pile of a love
Attaches like leeches,
Bites like Venus fly traps
And you're caught in what
Once was
First love.
The only good thing
Growing from this pile
Is your own resilience.

First love
That you thought would be
Your last love.
First love that never is.
First love that leaves,
First love that burns,
First love that breaks.

The flaw isn't
In loving the wrong one,
The flaw,
Instead, is in allowing yourself

To continue
To love them.

Ethel

The day my grandmother died,
 I was at the beach.
There was the most beautiful sunset,
like someone
Took out the clouds
And replaced them
With cotton candy.

If you knew my grandmother,
You know her favorite subject is God.
One of the earliest memories
I have of her was when I was six.
"Smile." She told me,
"But why? There's nothing to smile about."
I would say.
"Darling,
I've been around a lot longer than you have
And let me tell you,
There is everything to smile about.
The birds that sing you awake.
The sun that sets
And rises again.
The stars, the moon.
This is a beautiful world that
God has created for us."

"But grandma"
I would tell her,
"Grandma people die,
And babies cry
And homeless people live on the streets."
"I never said the world was
Fair, sweetheart.
But isn't it beautiful?"

When I heard about my grandmothers death

I did not cry, I laughed.
I laughed because I know
She is apart of this world
That she loved so much.
I see her in every sunrise and set.
I hear her voice in the chirping of the birds.
I see her beauty in the stars,
And her radiance in the moon.
When my grandmother died
I did not cry,
I laughed
Because I know that's what she would've wanted me to do.

And when a beautiful soul dies,
God lets them
paint the sky as their final goodbye.
The day my grandmother died,
there was the most beautiful sunset,
she had the most beautiful soul.
And no,
The world isn't always fair.
But oh God,
Isn't it beautiful?

What they Don't tell you

Despite what 4th period algebra
Will try to teach you,
Things in life
Do not always add up.
Two lovers do not always
Fit untarnished within one another.
The artist is not always
Looking to be saved.

Not every book will
Close with a beautiful final word.
You must learn
To leave things with loose ends.
You must learn
To leave people with unfinished stories.

Coughing Up Blood

We stopped breathing
and started heaving.
There's a fire
brewing in our lungs
but we can't stop coughing up blood
long enough to
Tell the stories
Of all the lives
We have lived.

Human Noise

I've always found that people
Tend to ask me questions like
"what is the meaning of life"
Or "do you believe in magic"
And "do you believe in God"
Expecting me to have all the answers
Because I have perfected the art
Of stringing secrets together
And performing them on stages.
But the truth is,
I don't know what the meaning of life is.
But I can tell you this,
I can tell you
That sometimes when I'm driving to the ocean
I get shivers down my spine
Because I am 70% water
And that is going home.
I can tell you
That on sunny days
I Turn the sprinklers on high
And run through them
Because a part of me refuses to grow up
I can tell you
That I've saved everything
I've ever gotten from a fortune cookie.

And the truth is,
I don't know anything about magic,
But I can tell you this,
I can tell you
That I believe in love
And fairytale endings
And the beauty of chance encounters.
I can tell you
That I have a bad habit
Looking strangers in the eye

Just to see if it's love at first sight.
I don't know much about magic
But I can tell you this,
I can tell you that I believe in love
And I think that's pretty damn close.

The truth is,
I've always had a hard time
Believing in things I could not see
So I can't tell you
If I believe in God
I can't tell you
If I believe in magic
And I can't tell you
What I think the meaning of life is
But the truth is,
I believe in the kindness of strangers
And that's the closest to God I've ever gotten.

I can tell you that all I
Wanted to be when I was younger
Was everything.
I can tell you
That I've always had
A Deep and profound love
For the things that we don't like to talk about
In earthquakes,
Blackouts,
And how it feels to go to bed
After you've just gotten your
Heart broken.

And I don't know much
About having faith and abstract ideas,
But I can tell you this,
I can tell you that one time
I witnessed a ladybug land in the palm
Of a small kid's hand,

And I watched as he carried it
To a flower,
And I can tell you,
That's all I know about purity.

I don't have all the answers
Because most days
I'm still asking questions myself,
So I don't quite know
What the meaning of life is.
But I can tell you this,
I can tell you
That I have a friend that once loved a girl
Who had no intention of loving them back
And that's all I have to say
About fear.
That's all I have to say
About life.
And that's all I have to say
About love.

And so,
I don't know much
Of anything, really,
But I do know
A whole lot
About nothing much at all.

P.S. Don't forget to dance in the rain.

About the Author

Lauren Waites is a spoken word poet and short story writer rooted in Cerritos, California. At a young age, she found a passion for words and the way the human spirit can be conveyed through text. She hopes, more than anything, that this work will evoke its readers to listen carefully to the things we talk about at night, to love recklessly, and to make a little more noise.

Made in the USA
San Bernardino, CA
09 September 2016